Glorious Angels

Glorious Angels

A CELEBRATION OF CHILDREN

WALTER DEAN MYERS

HarperCollins*Publishers*

ALSO BY WALTER DEAN MYERS

Brown Angels
An Album of Pictures and Verse

Scorpions

The Mouse Rap

Now Is Your Time!
The African-American Struggle for Freedom

The Righteous Revenge of Artemis Bonner

The Story of the Three Kingdoms
Illustrated by Ashley Bryan

Photograph on page 12 "The Gift of Love," is copyrighted by Donna Mussenden VanDerZee. The photograph "The Gift of Love," of Claire D. Slater Taylor, her sister Gwendolyn Slater Spencer, and her aunt Laurabelle Slater on page 12 is used by permission of Claire Taylor.

Pictures on pages 27 and 36 used by permission of the National Park Service.

Library of Congress Cataloging-in-Publication Data
Myers, Walter Dean, date.
  Glorious angels : a celebration of children / Walter Dean Myers.
    p.   cm.
  Summary: A collection of poems and antique photographs depicting children of many different nationalities.
  ISBN 0-06-024822-X. — ISBN 0-06-024823-8 (lib. bdg.)
  1. Children—Juvenile poetry. 2. Children's poetry, American.
3. Children—Pictorial works—Juvenile literature. [1. Children—
Poetry. 2. American poetry.] I. Title.
PS3563.Y48G56 1995   94-49699
811'.54—dc20   CIP
                                                            AC

2 3 4 5 6 7 8 9 10
◆

Glorious Angels

hildren remind us of those days when the world was a place of wonder and excitement, a time when love was freely given and play was a serious part of life. Photographs also remind us of those days.

The children in these photographs are full of promise and excitement. Their early steps are sometimes hesitant, sometimes reckless, but they represent all that humankind can be. When we celebrate these children we celebrate ourselves. We celebrate life.

Since my first book of antique photographs and verse, *Brown Angels,* was published, people have been sending me photographs of themselves, of their parents, grandparents, and even great-grandparents as children. Others have created their own books from their own family photograph collections. Teachers have had their classes make books, with students bringing in photographs and writing their own poetry. Each picture that comes to me, each carefully constructed book, is precious to me, as is each child in each photograph.

Children throughout the world recognize other children. Even babies react with joy when they see another baby. The nationality or race of the child never matters. This book reflects that idea, and that the experience of childhood is universal and marvelous.

Some of the photographs come from even dustier attics than the ones I searched through for *Brown Angels*, others come from dealers around the world who know me as the American who "collects children." I am proud to be so known and to share these photographs with you.

Walter Dean Myers

The Mother

Celebrate this child

This tender vessel

of blessed innocence

This lifter

of my joyful heart

This angel

of my dreams come true

Celebrate these tiny fingers

These precious eyes

that glance into

my very soul and,

in rich delight

Exalt the gifts I bring

Celebrate these rosy lips

that curl in patient smiles

So wide I am encircled,

lost . . .

sweetly enrapt in love

Celebrate this child

of mine

G. Morita 壹萬賣 大阪本町御常備懸物繪模様西門北

守田昌司

The Father

Celebrate this child

This new-moon face shining

on yesterday and tomorrow

This gentle dancer moving

to the rhythm of my heart

Celebrate this spring
This image of tender blossom
This promise of new harvest
Green shoot in a snowy field

Celebrate this hope

This vessel that welcomes life

This fragile keeper of breath

Holding out all

I was thought to be

Celebrate this child

The Village

Let us celebrate the children

Let us spin mysteries

for their minds

and wonders for their hearts

Let us bring love

and sing love and

ring garlands of love

around them

Let us grease their ashy knees

with hosannas

and braid dignity

into curly hair

Let us be warriors

for the children

Let us parade them to

tambourine and tabla

Sprinkling hallelujahs

in their paths

Let the gospel choir

shout praises unto them

And the saints of God

feed them kola nuts and honey

As the elders warm them

with their smiles

Let us make holidays

and days of praise

and words that raise them

to the heavens

Let us celebrate

each child as best

most adored,

Most surely blessed

Let us turn them
to the moon and stars
and name them
Glorious and Wonderful
Wonderful
and forever Glorious

Let us hear

the questions in their tears

And let us hear

them with our hearts

In the beginning

Let us celebrate the children

and bring them peace

Then let us speak love

to them and love again

In every waking breath

Let us celebrate the children